THE INSIDER'S GUIDE TO FISHING

FRESHWATER FISHING LIKE A PRO

DWAYNE HICKS

ROSEN PUBLISHING

Published in 2024 by The Rosen Publishing Group, Inc.
2544 Clinton Street, Buffalo, NY 14224

Portions of this work were originally authored by Judy Monroe Peterson and published as *Fishing in Lakes and Ponds*. All new material in this edition was authored by Dwayne Hicks.

Editor: Greg Roza
Designer: Michael Flynn

Cataloging-in-Publication Data

Names: Hicks, Dwayne.
Title: Freshwater fishing like a pro / Dwayne Hicks.
Description: New York : Rosen Publishing, 2024. | Series: The insider's guide to fishing | Includes glossary and index.
Identifiers: ISBN 9781499476002 (pbk.) | ISBN 9781499476019 (library bound) | ISBN 9781499476026 (ebook)
Subjects: LCSH: Fishing--Juvenile literature. | Freshwater fishes--Juvenile literature.
Classification: LCC SH445.H55 2024 | DDC 799.1'1--dc23

Some of the images in this book illustrate individuals who are models. The depictions do not imply actual situations or events.

Manufactured in the United States of America

CPSIA Compliance Information: Batch #CWRYA24. For further information, contact Rosen Publishing at 1-800-237-9932.

CONTENTS

INTRODUCTION

About 71 percent of Earth's surface is covered with water; a staggering 96.5 percent of this water is salty ocean water. Fresh water makes up just 3.5 percent of all the water on Earth. Much of this fresh water is deep underground or frozen in glaciers. This leaves just 1.2 percent as surface fresh water, which sustains countless forms of life including people, plants, and microorganisms. Luckily, this tiny percentage of fresh water provides plenty of sources for the freshwater fishers of the world!

Millions of people worldwide enjoy fishing in a wide variety of lakes, ponds, and rivers. A lake is a body of water surrounded by land. Many natural lakes are enlarged sections of rivers or creeks. River curves that became separated from the main river over time are called oxbow lakes. Some lakes are made from melting snow or rain that runs off from the surrounding area. A pond is a body of still freshwater and is smaller than a lake. Natural underwater springs create many ponds, and sometimes people create their own ponds.

Anglers—fishers who use a rod and line—catch many kinds of freshwater fish in lakes and ponds. Unlike oceans and seas, almost all inland lakes and ponds contain little or no salt. Many people search for small fish called panfish. This includes sunfish (sunnies), crappies, bluegills, and perch. Others prefer larger fish such as walleyes, northern pike, and muskellunge (muskies).

Freshwater fishing is a pastime enjoyed by people of all ages in North America. Many anglers make frequent trips to nearby lakes and ponds. Others take longer trips to large lakes so they can catch a particular type of freshwater fish. Many people use rods, reels, and other equipment, which allows for a variety of angling methods. However, people can fish in lakes and ponds using simple equipment such as a cane pole. The type of equipment used to catch fish can depend on the type of fish, the location, and the angler's personal preferences.

Fishing takes patience, knowledge, and skill. Anglers use different strategies to outwit freshwater fish. They use bait based on the habits of particular types of fish—and sometimes the places where these fish live. Zones are layers of different temperatures of water in a lake or pond that separate different fish habitats. Small fish are usually found in the shallow, warmer water zone. Larger fish are often found in the open water zone. Some fish live only in the deeper, colder water zone.

Anglers need to be aware of state and provincial fishing laws before they even head out on a fishing trip. All anglers need to know and follow regulations. Laws vary from state to state. Sometimes states reserve certain lakes for releasing caught fish. All states and provinces require anglers to buy a fishing license. State and federal laws exist to avoid the overharvesting and extinction of freshwater fish. To manage their fish populations, states have

Freshwater fishing can take many forms. This teen is fishing from a dock. You can fish from the shore, or even wade into the body of water, if you have the right tools.

seasons for each type of fish. People can legally keep a particular fish during its season.

By purchasing licenses and paying taxes on fishing gear, anglers provide money to the states to enforce fishing laws. This money is also used to manage fishing and boating access of lakes, ponds, and rivers and to protect freshwater fishing habitats. State agencies also work to stop invasive species from taking over fishing sources. The federal government offers many freshwater fishing opportunities through its National Wildlife Refuge fishing programs. The National Fish Hatchery System allows fishing at or near many hatcheries.

Some fishers prefer the peace and quiet of fishing alone. However, others enjoy fishing with friends and family. Fishing is an activity that pairs well with boating, camping, picnicking, hiking, or viewing wildlife. Some anglers like the challenge of finding and landing big fish and then releasing them back into the lake or pond after taking a photograph. Other people catch fish to preserve and save as trophies. Many kinds of freshwater fish are both tasty and nutritious, and some people make a good living from catching and selling edible fish.

Whether you're looking for a peaceful afternoon of fishing or an extensive fishing trip with family and friends, there's a place for that! Freshwater fishing in lakes, ponds, rivers, and creeks has long been a popular activity in the United States, Canada, and around the world.

CHAPTER 1

RESPONSIBLE FISHING

People love to fish for various reasons. Some love the sporting nature of the activity. It can be a great accomplishment to land a large, powerful fish! Some prefer to spend a quiet afternoon on a placid lake, fishing for walleyes, pike, and muskies and releasing the fish back into the water. This is called catch-and-release fishing. Regardless of the reason you enjoy fishing, it's essential for all anglers to be responsible. Your health and safety are most important. Fishers should prepare to be safe and comfortable in the outdoors, including near or on water. Bad weather can suddenly develop without warning. People can get painful sunburns or get caught on a fishhook. Safe anglers avoid and help prevent accidents.

Before you even leave for a fishing trip, it's important to let someone know where you'll be fishing and when you'll return. In addition, always keep the telephone number for the local wildlife management office stored in your cell phone. If an accident does happen, you can call for help quickly.

WEATHER AND WATER SAFETY

When planning a fishing trip, check the weather forecast and be prepared for all kinds of weather. Even if the forecast seems OK, keep an eye out for unexpected wind, rain, and snow. It's a good idea to take a waterproof radio to listen to weather forecasts when you're on longer trips. Thick, gray clouds rolling in or sudden gusts of cold air signal an approaching storm. If you ever hear thunder or see lightning, get to safety right away. If a storm approaches, people in boats should head for shore. Stay away from tall trees and move to low ground in case there are nearby lightning strikes. Wearing rainwear and other items can help keep people from getting wet and chilled.

Water safety is crucial for people who like to fish on boats and docks. Keep your boat at a safe speed and watch wave conditions. Be watchful for sandbars, rocks, and underwater trees that could snag the boat. It's important for fishers to stay away from litter that could cut or entangle their fishing equipment or the boat motor. It should also be mentioned that people should never throw garbage into the water or around the dock or shore. This is unfair to others and could cause damage, or harm, in many ways. Stray hooks and fishing line can cause a lot of problems for people and wildlife.

Most states require that anglers wear flotation gear while on the water. These life vests, often called personal protection devices (PPDs), are lightweight and do not restrict people's movements. Flotation devices should be worn at all times, whether anglers are on a boat or a dock.

Don't try to fish from docks that are in disrepair. Before wading into water, check for sharp drop-offs and areas with powerful undercurrents. Be careful to take one step at a time because it can be slippery along banks. Wading with rubber boots or tennis shoes protects the feet from sharp pieces of debris such as broken glass. Special fishing boots called waders will keep most of your body dry while you're standing in a lake, pond, or river.

SAFETY FIRST

Always walk, never run, when around slippery areas. Fishers should wear flotation devices when they are on docks or on the banks of lakes or ponds. All fishing boats must have U.S. Coast Guard–approved inflatable life jackets for everyone aboard. Inflatable life jackets keep people face up with their head above the water and afloat. These devices are available in many sizes. They also come in different styles and colors.

BE PREPARED!

Cuts, scrapes, and bruises happen when you're on a fishing trip. Treating injuries right away lessens the chance of wounds becoming infected and helps keep fishers from ending their trip too soon.

A basic first-aid kit can allow people to get immediate treatment for minor injuries. You can buy a kit for fishing trips or make your own using a small, waterproof container. A first-aid kit should contain bandages of different sizes, antibiotic ointment, safety scissors, gauze, medical tape, and cleansing towelettes (wet wipes) or hand sanitizer.

An over-the-counter pain reliever such as acetaminophen or ibuprofen can help lessen the pain from an injury or headache. Other items that can come in handy are tweezers, a small bottle of water to rinse wounds, and a cold pack to help reduce swelling caused by an injury. Extra insect repellent and sunblock lotion are also good to include in the kit.

For more urgent emergencies, people might need to contact medical help. Always bring a cell phone and a charger with you, especially if your trip lasts more than one day.

The best way to avoid injuries in the first place is to practice responsible fishing. Always be aware of the people around you when casting or baiting a hook. Never leave garbage or fishing gear lying on the ground where people are walking and fishing. Bring sunscreen and a hat with a brim to avoid sunburn. Don't forget the PPDs!

Make sure you have enough floatation life vests for everyone on the trip, no matter how old they are.

Docks near water can be very slippery at any time, and in the winter, they may be covered with ice. Always wear appropriate shoes or boots when fishing from a dock.

When fishing, you should wear a billed hat or cap and polarized sunglasses. A hat protects you from the sun's hot rays. It also helps protect you from getting hooked if another angler makes a bad cast. Wearing polarized sunglasses protects your eyes and helps you spot fish. You can also protect yourself with sunscreen and lip balm. Cover your face, neck, ears, the back of your hands, legs, and other skin exposed to the sun with a waterproof sunscreen that has a sun protection factor (SPF) of 15 or higher. Sunburns are more likely to happen during the middle of the day when the sun is the hottest and reflects off the water. Don't forget the insect repellent to ward off mosquitoes, flies, and bees.

It's important to take breaks to stay hydrated and prevent heatstroke (effects of too much heat). Be sure to pack a lunch as well as cold water and other healthy drinks. Many sodas (soft drinks) contain caffeine and increase the likelihood of becoming dehydrated. Energy bars, fruit, nuts, and other healthy snacks are good choices.

Before going fishing, savvy fishers check the weather forecast and wear the right clothing. When fishing in warm or hot weather, it's a good idea to bring rain gear as the weather can change quickly. Anglers should bring warmer clothing in case the weather turns cold. When fishing in cold weather, anglers will want to dress in layers and wear a warm hat. To keep dry, the outer layer needs to be waterproof. Underneath, people can wear layers of comfortable, warm clothing.

EQUIPMENT SAFETY

Safe use of fishing equipment can help you avoid accidents. Never point your fishing rod toward the sky when you are walking; keep it pointed toward the ground. When casting, watch for people behind, on the sides, and in front of you. An overhead cast is safer than side casts. Overhead casts can help anglers avoid crossing or tangling their fishing line with that of someone else.

Hooks need to be sharp to hang on to fish. They require careful attention when baiting and all other times. Fishers should not grab a fish where it's hooked. Fish wiggle when hooked, and the hook can get caught in your hand. It's similarly important to remove hooks from fish carefully. The fish can wiggle around, and they are often very slippery. Hooks can also become lodged in a fish's throat or eye. For this reason, many fishers use barbless hooks, or they cut the barbs off before using hooks, making them easier and safer to remove.

Single hooks, which are used for bait, have just one hook. Treble hooks have three hooks and are most often used with lures.

It's important to always handle fish carefully and avoid the mouth and spines. Some fish have sharp fins on their backs. Perch and other fish have sharp gill covers. Gills are openings on a fish's sides that allow the fish to breathe dissolved oxygen as it swims through water.

Taking care of your equipment and preparing it for a trip will help avoid problems during the trip. Keep your fishing knives sharp and cover the blades when the knives are not in use. You should clean your rods, reels, hooks, lures, and other fishing equipment after a fishing trip. That way it's ready to go for the next trip. Fishers should watch for rough spots on rods because they will cause extra wear on the line. You don't want your line to break as you're reeling in a fish!

TREBLE HOOKS

RULES AND REGULATIONS

Every state and province requires anglers over a certain age to buy a fishing license. The ages range from as young as 10 in Arizona to 18 in Alaska and Indiana. In Canada, people 16 years and older generally need to buy a license. People who are traveling can often purchase a license that is good for one or more days.

Fishing licenses may be purchased from the local department of environmental conservation, sporting goods stores, bait shops, or the state's department of natural resources. You may be able to apply for a fishing license online, but you may need a driver's license to do so. Anglers must know and follow the fishing laws for the state. The laws include limits, legal hours, license requirements, seasons, any special regulations, and allowable gear. Fishing regulations differ for each state. People can obtain the regulations wherever they purchase fishing licenses.

Many states have restrictions regarding the use of lures, hooks, and bait for certain waters. States control the number of fish that can be taken in one day and during a season for fishing in lakes and ponds. The limits may be different for each type of fish and the time of year. Other laws require that people take only fish of a specific size. Anglers are encouraged to release fish they catch if the fish will not be eaten. Mature fish will continue to reproduce, so when they are released, they help keep the fish populations higher.

It's important to follow the rules regarding fishing limits. Taking too many fish, or fish that are too big or small, can affect fish populations and make fishing harder in the future.

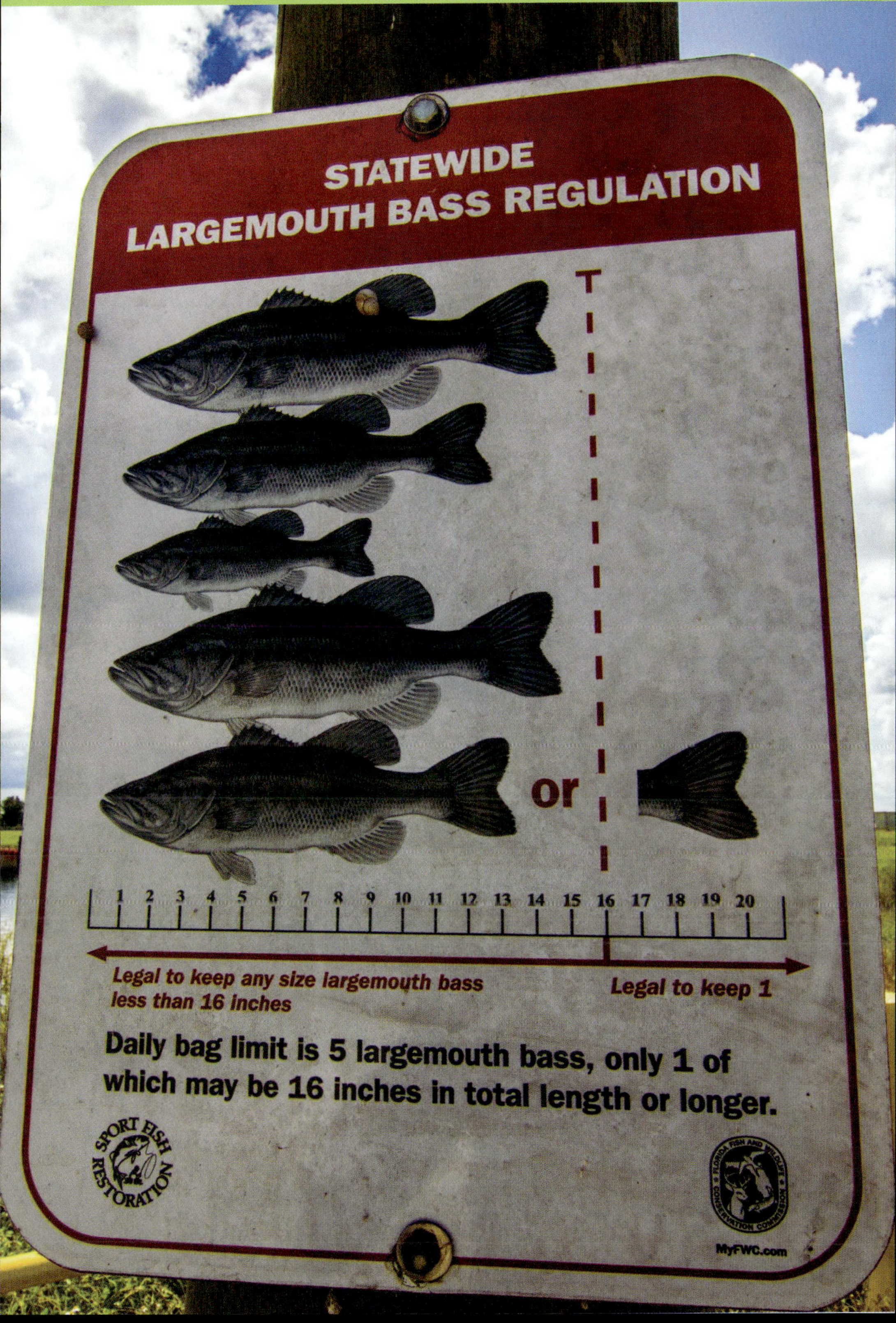
STATEWIDE
LARGEMOUTH BASS REGULATION
or
1 2 3 4 5 6 7 8 9 10 11 12 13 14 15 16 17 18 19 20
Legal to keep any size largemouth bass less than 16 inches
Legal to keep 1
Daily bag limit is 5 largemouth bass, only 1 of which may be 16 inches in total length or longer.
SPORT FISH RESTORATION
FLORIDA FISH AND WILDLIFE CONSERVATION COMMISSION
MyFWC.com

GOOD SPORTSMANSHIP

Good sportsmanship while fishing is important for several reasons. It's important to follow the license requirements for the number and size of fish that one fisher can catch. Doing otherwise is unfair to other fishers. Other rules or laws should also be observed, such as following the hours when a body of water is open for fishing.

Fishers show good sportsmanship when they're respectful of other people and their property. Never fish on private land without the permission of the landowner. It's illegal to trespass on others' property. You may come across other people enjoying the land and wildlife, such as hikers, bird watchers, and campers. Fishers need to respect swimmers, boaters, and other anglers so that these people can also enjoy their activities on the water. When anglers fish from docks or boats, they should keep some distance between them and others. This helps avoid injuries and accidents.

Before leaving the lake or pond, be sure to pack your bait containers and any trash you have and dispose of them properly. Some fishing facilities will provide trash cans and an area to clean the fish you catch. If there are no trash cans or cleaning areas, take your garbage home and dispose of it there. You may need to keep your fish on ice until you can get home to clean them.

Never throw garbage or fish guts on the ground, deck, or in the water. Fish, birds, and small animals can swallow discarded plastic lures, fishing line, and hooks and then die. Anglers need to treat public and private property as if it were their own. Public lands belong to everyone and should be protected for everyone's use or access.

Garbage left behind by careless fishers can cause harm to other people and wildlife. Always clean up after yourself!

KNOW THE LOCATION

Always learn all you can about the area where you plan to fish. Never fish in areas where it's prohibited. Areas might be off limits to fishing to protect wildlife, vegetation, or people. The shorelines of some lakes and ponds are privately owned. Pay attention to signage and other indications that an area is off limits to public fishing.

You may want to ask a local fisher where the best places are. They may be able to point out not only a good body of water but possibly even the best spots on that body of water. You may get good advice from locals at a bait shop or store that sells fishing gear.

When you find a good fishing spot, make a note of its location. Also note what time the fish were biting, the weather conditions, and the bait used. This information will help when planning future fishing trips.

SAFE EATING

Freshwater fish that are commonly caught for eating can contain a variety of contaminants (poisons) that may make people sick. Typical contaminants include lead and mercury, which often come from agricultural and manufacturing runoff. Other chemicals, such as polychlorinated biphenyls (PCBs), chlordane, and DDT, have been banned in the United States. However, they last a long time in the mud beneath the water. Small fish eat the dangerous chemicals that have settled in the mud. Bigger fish, such as walleyes, northern pike, and muskies, eat smaller fish and the contaminants are passed along to them. When people catch and eat these fish, the chemicals are passed along again.

Anglers should follow the public postings that recommend which fish and how much of that fish can be safely eaten. Always check the websites of local and state departments of natural resources. They will list the lakes and rivers that are polluted, as well as the limits on fish.

Many communities have local fishing clubs you can join. That way you can find the best local fishing spots while making new friends who enjoy similar activities.

CHAPTER 2

FRESHWATER FISHING EQUIPMENT

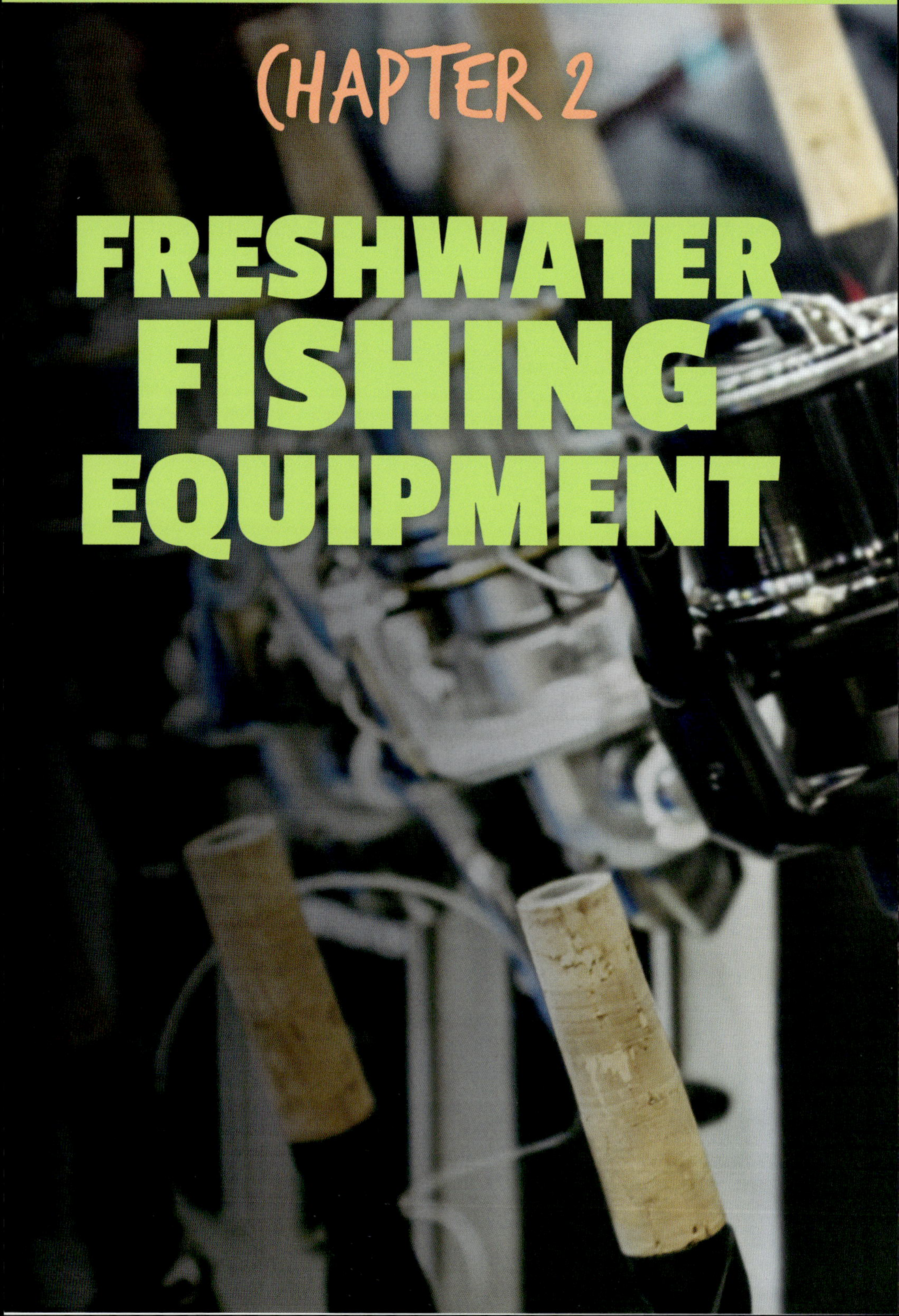

Although there's a multitude of fishing equipment one can purchase—hooks and lures and boats and sonar—anglers really only need three basic tools to catch fish in lakes, ponds, rivers, and creeks: a rod, a reel, and fishing line. They also need hooks on the end of the fishing line to attach their bait. Other equipment includes bobbers, weights, and lures.

Fishing equipment is called tackle. Most of these items fit inside a carrying case called a tackle box. People organize and store their equipment in a tackle box and take it when they go fishing. The type of equipment needed by the anglers depends on the type of fish they plan to catch.

A freshwater fisher may not need all the supplies shown here. However, some supplies are needed for specific fish or locations.

THE BASICS

Angling can't be done without a fishing rod, and most rods are equipped with a reel for winding fishing line. Rods are tapered poles of various thicknesses and lengths. Materials such as fiberglass, graphite, and carbon fiber are popular choices for rods because they are strong, lightweight, and flexible. Fishing rods are commonly 5 to 7 feet (1.5 to 2.1 m) long. A shorter rod is best for shorter, more accurate casts. A longer rod allows for casting farther out into the water.

Different rods are designed for different purposes. People who prefer panfish require short, fast-action rods that bend at the tip. Slow-action rods, on the other hand, bend closer to the reel and handle. These rods are stronger, longer, and more flexible. They are often used to catch large walleyes, northern pike, and muskies. Many people choose medium-action rods when fishing for various species of fish in lakes and ponds. These rods bend in the middle.

Reels are spools that neatly store unused line. They allow anglers to control the line as well as the bait or lure on the end of the line. People release line when casting and retrieve line by turning the reel's handle. Most reels feature a device that controls the tension (tightness) of the line on the spool while fishing.

The most popular types of reels on the market for freshwater fishing are spinning and spincast reels. Spinning reels have an open-faced spool mounted on the reel that does not turn when the line is cast or retrieved. The line comes off the open end of the spool while the fisher is casting. Spinning reels have a handle and a bail to retrieve line or allow line to come off the spool. The bail winds the line around the spool. The spool turns only when the fish pulls on the line hard enough to overcome the drag.

With some basic fishing gear, you can find success fishing from docks and shores. Just make sure fishing isn't prohibited there!

FISHING WITH BAMBOO?

As one of the oldest forms of fishing, cane pole fishing is still popular today. Cane poles are often made from dried bamboo or a sapling tree. They don't have reels. Rather, anglers attach strong fishing line to one end of the pole. Cane poles are inexpensive and a good choice for beginning anglers for fishing in lakes and ponds.

At about 8 feet (2.4 m) in length, cane poles are often longer than standard rods for freshwater fishing. A cane pole allows anglers to feel the slightest nibble of a fish. A disadvantage of this type of fishing is that the line is much shorter and anglers can't cast their bait a longer distance from shore. All the casts must be close. Because people cannot cast a long distance with a cane pole, they place the bait in precise spots. This practice allows them to target close areas with pinpoint accuracy (right next to a lily pad, for example). Pole fishing is efficient with the use of bobbers for panfish.

Spincast reels have a hood or cap covering a spool. Line comes off the spool and passes through a hole in the hood or cap. They include a button to release line from the spool during casting and when retrieving the line. A device winds the line evenly onto the spool and prevents it from tangling.

FISHING LINE

It would be difficult to go fishing without fishing line! Monofilament lines are popular for people who fish in lakes, ponds, and rivers. These single, strong strands of plastic fibers are used on spinning and spincast reels and come in many thicknesses and lengths. Monofilament is

Spinning and spincast reels are just two kinds.
Others include baitcasting, trolling, and fly-fishing reels.

usually clear or tinted to match the color of the water so fish have trouble seeing it. Lightweight monofilament of 6-pound test works well for panfish. This means that six pounds (2.7 kilograms) of pressure can be put on the line before it breaks. Anglers use heavier, stronger lines to catch larger freshwater fish, such as walleyes, muskies, and northern pike. The thicker the monofilament is, the more weight it can hold. However, it's more difficult to cast with thicker line.

HOOKS

Hooks are strong, metal, and very sharp. They range in size from 1 (large) to 22 (small). People fishing in lakes and ponds typically find that hook sizes 14 to 16 work well for most fish. However, a size 6 to 10 hook is best for panfish.

Hooks can be used individually. You can buy hooks in packs of 10 or by the hundreds! Many fisheries specify that fishers should use barbless hooks, especially if a catch-and-release policy is in effect. A barb holds the hook in place when a fish is caught but is difficult to remove without damaging the fish. You can buy barbless hooks, or you can carefully snip the barbs off your hooks with a pair of needle-nose pliers.

BAIT

Anglers use a variety of natural and artificial bait to catch fish. Panfish, walleyes, muskies, and northern pike feed on smaller fish and other small animals including crayfish, waterfowl, and rodents. Small fish such as minnows are a perfect choice. Other natural bait includes worms, leeches, insects, frogs, corn, cheese, and popcorn. To attract and catch panfish, minnows and worms should be threaded on

TYING THE UNI-KNOT

It's a good idea to practice how to properly attach hooks to monofilament. Always take your time and be careful of the sharp end of the hook. Many fishing injuries occur when people are rushing or not paying attention.

Perhaps the most common knot used in fishing is called the uni-knot. Here's how to do it!

- Feed the monofilament through the eye (hole) of the hook. Make a loop with the line as shown in the diagram.
- Wrap the line around the two sections of line five or six times while leaving the loop free.
- Wet the monofilament and pull the end of the line. This will cause the loop to tighten and form a knot.
- Slide knot down to the eye to finish tightening. Use scissors to remove any excess line.

HOW TO TIE A UNI-KNOT

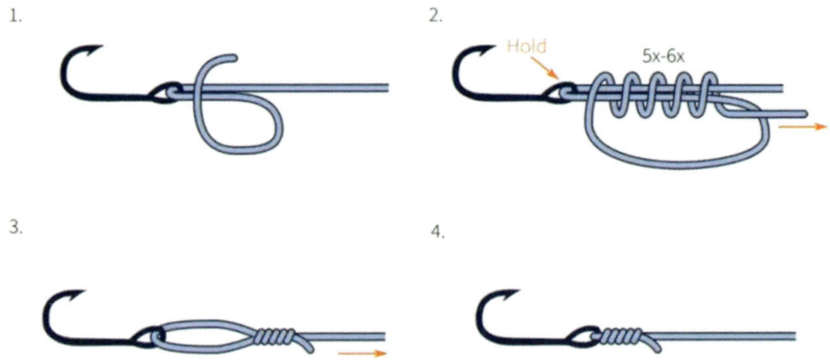

a hook. If threaded correctly, the minnow will swim and only the end of the worm will dangle in the water. Some fishers prefer to use live bait so their natural movements attract fish.

LURES

Lures are artificial bait that can be reused. Most lures are designed to look and move like a fish's prey. Some are made to look just like a swimming frog! Lures come in thousands of shapes and sizes. Most are made of plastic, rubber, metal, or wood. Lures can come with a single hook for catching smaller fish or up to nine grouped hooks for catching larger, stronger fish.

Lures come in many shapes, sizes, and colors.

Metal spinners and spoons are popular lures. Spinners, as the name suggests, spin in the water and reflect light as the lure is retrieved. The noise, light, and movement attract fish. Spoons wobble when they are pulled through the water. They are often colorfully painted, and some are shiny metal to reflect light. Anglers use spoons weighing 1/16 ounce (1.8 g) for small panfish. Larger spoons are required for walleyes, northern pike, and muskies. Crank baits and poppers are also popular lures when fishing on lakes and ponds. By tying feathers and string to a steel hook, people try to create artificial lures that resemble an insect or small animal. These lures are usually called flies. Some people consider creating flies to be an art form.

IN THE TACKLE BOX

Many fishers carry their supplies in a convenient tackle box. These come in varying sizes. Most have compartments to keep hooks and lures safely organized. Some feature trays that unfold to provide more room for storage.

What else do anglers store in their tackle box? Sinkers are tiny weights that are tied to the line near the hook so that the bait sinks to the correct depth in a lake or pond. Bobbers are light, hollow objects attached to the line. They float on the surface of the water. They wiggle or bob up and down when a fish nibbles or strikes at the bait or lure. Using a bobber allows the angler to place the line at a greater distance from the shoreline or boat.

Leaders are thin wire lines that attach between a swivel on the end of the line and the hook. Swivels allow the bait attached to the leader to turn freely, which keeps the line from twisting. Steel leaders can also stop fish with

A stocked tackle box should contain the items needed to catch a variety of fish, but it may also hold tools, first-aid supplies, and more.

sharp teeth, such as northern pike and muskie, from biting through the line.

Anglers often need a few specific tools. Most carry at least one pocketknife and nail clippers. These tools come in handy to cut fishing line and other gear. In addition, anglers can remove hooks from the mouth or stomach of a caught fish with forceps or pliers. A bait box is useful for storing bait. Other useful tools may include scissors, a filleting knife, a fishing net, and a scale for weighing your catch.

Fishing is an outdoor wilderness activity. Anglers need to think of their own safety. Dress for the weather! If it's cold and rainy, you will want to wear layers and a waterproof jacket. Waders are tall, waterproof boots or pants that keep anglers dry when they're standing in a lake or river. If it's hot and sunny, you will need sunscreen and a hat.

GETTING HIGH TECH

As you've already read, you can go fishing with a bamboo pole, a fishing line, and a hook. Some people can make these from items found in nature. A thin, flexible branch can be used as a pole. Fishing line can be made from plant fiber braided together. Sharp plant thorns can be used as makeshift hooks.

However, this is the 21st century! Traditional fishing techniques have been transformed by modern technology. Even a simple rowboat or canoe can be considered technology to improve your chances of catching freshwater fish. A watercraft provides access to deep areas of a lake or to a submerged (beneath the surface of the water) island. You don't need to buy a boat, either. You can rent one!

You can sometimes access a topographical lake map to locate fishing spots. The topography of the bottom of a lake or pond is important because it can identify where fish are likely to rest or feed. Additional electronic devices such as depth finders and global positioning systems (GPS) are also useful. Depth finders use sonar to help locate fish. They display the location of fish on a screen. After they find fish, people can use GPS coordinates to mark the location for future fishing. Although these electronic tools might be expensive, some shops will rent them to anglers.

CHAPTER 3

MEET THE FRESHWATER FISH

Many of the lakes and ponds in the United States and southern Canada are home to numerous species of freshwater fish, including panfish, walleyes, northern pike, and muskies. Anglers need to learn how to correctly identify their fish. They also must learn the habits and behavior of the different types of fish. Habits, or predictable animal behaviors, include finding comfortable water temperatures, feeding, resting, spawning, and hiding from predators under cover.

The chances of catching fish increase as people learn more about fish characteristics and feeding habits. Water temperature has an important effect on the hunger and activity of freshwater fish. Fish move to different depths to locate comfortable temperatures. Experienced fishers are patient and may need to change methods and bait to catch fish.

The term "panfish" includes numerous species, including bluegills, sunfish, crappies, and some kinds of perch. The term refers to edible freshwater fish that can fit in a frying pan.

PANFISH

Panfish are smaller freshwater fish that are plentiful across the United States. They can weigh as much as 1 pound (450 g) but usually weigh less. Panfish average 6 to 8 inches (15 to 20 cm) in length. Many panfish prefer to live near warm shorelines that feature places to hide such as lily pads, logs, sunken trees, boat docks, and weeds. Panfish eat in early morning and dusk, so these are the best times to search for them. In the spring, during spawning season, panfish are hungry and gather near shore. They also bite well most of the summer and early fall.

Pumpkinseed sunfish and bluegills live near warm shorelines. Pumpkinseeds have a small mouth, an orange breast and belly, and an ear flap with a bright red or orange spot. Bluegills have a small mouth and a light-yellow belly. Their upper body is olive green, dark bands circle the back, and they have a dark area near the tail. Both sunfish and bluegills eat insects, mollusks, snails, and other small fish.

Crappies are silvery olive with a high fin on the back and belly. Black crappies have dark green spots, and dark green-white crappies have bands of dark green speckles on their body. Crappies and yellow perch both have similar diets; they eat insects, spiders, snails, worms, fish eggs, and small fish. Yellow perch are long, slender fish with a large mouth and two top fins. Their golden yellow body has dark bands down the sides, and their belly is white or yellow. Perch often swim in schools.

Anglers catch many kinds of panfish using worms or crickets as bait. To keep panfish from stealing the bait, weave the worm on the hook and leave a little of the tail dangling in the water. Small leeches and artificial insects also work well as bait. Dropping bait into the water while still-fishing is probably the easiest way to catch panfish, but slow trolling and drifting are techniques that work well too.

Still-fishing is when fishers use lightweight line, small weights, small bobbers, and sizes 6- to 10-long shank hooks. They drop the line into the water and allow the bait to float at a certain depth. Anglers jiggle the bobber to move the worm around in the water. The movement catches the fish's eye. When a panfish latches on to the bait, anglers set the hook firmly with a hard, quick snap of the wrist.

Walleyes swim in schools, so when one of them is caught, there's usually more to be caught! Walleyes are a popular fish because their white meat is flaky and delicious.

WALLEYES

Large populations of walleyes commonly live in lakes in Minnesota, Wisconsin, Ohio, Michigan, and much of Canada. A full-grown walleye typically weighs 1 to 8 pounds (0.4 to 3.6 kg) in the northern states and 15 to 20 pounds (6.8 to 9 kg) in the southern states. Walleye color varies, but most are gold or olive with a white belly. They have a dark mark near the tail and a white tip on the lower tail. Their large, silvery eyes glow in the dark. Walleyes feed mostly on small fish, insects, crayfish, and worms. They often travel in schools and prefer clear, cool waters with sandy or rocky bottoms. To look for food, walleyes search through rock piles, gravel bars, coral reefs, and weeds.

Walleyes often gather when the sun is setting or when the water is muddy due to wind or weather. During these times, slow trolling with artificial lures or shiners (large minnows) is a successful fishing technique. This method requires a boat with legally placed lights on the bow and stern. Anglers use sonar to locate walleyes, or they may use trolling lures to catch them in deep water.

Walleyes are also caught by still-fishing and drifting. Good bait for these methods includes minnows, jigs with worms, and spinners. Walleyes aren't that picky, and they will also go after other bait such as night crawlers and leeches. A 12-pound (5.4 kg) line or less is used, along with a sinker so that the hook with bait reaches the bottom of a lake. When a walleye picks up the bait, it slowly swims away. When fishers feel a slight tug on their line, they should release the line until the walleye stops, then quickly reel up the line to set the hook.

FINDING BAIT

Worms are excellent bait for panfish. Luckily, worms are plentiful in most areas. Anglers can collect their own night crawlers by looking for them on the soil with flashlights right after dark. Worms are often easy to find on rainy days, as well. To enhance the collection of night crawlers, some people water their lawns heavily, which drives the worms to the top of the soil. Anglers can find red worms by spading and turning over rich soil. Many fishing shops and convenience stores also sell bait—some even have bait vending machines!

Walleyes, northern pike, muskies, and other larger fish eat fry (small, juvenile fish) and minnows. Using live bait fish, such as minnows, is an effective way to catch fish in lakes and ponds. Although anglers can buy minnows, they can also catch their own. To do this, they need to buy minnow traps. People place bread or corn in the traps, which attracts the minnows. Some walleyes will even eat the fry (juvenile fish) of their own species. However, anglers need to be aware that catching and using the fry of game fish as bait is illegal in all states.

NORTHERN PIKE

Northern pike are large, spear-shaped freshwater fish. They are referred to as a northern, a pike, or a northern pike. They are green or black with a white or yellow belly. This fish has white or light-yellow spots on its sides with fins that are tipped in orange. Rows of razor-sharp teeth line its mouth.

A northern pike can grow to more than 3 feet (1 m) long and weigh more than 20 pounds (9 kg).

While small fish often prefer to live in warm, shallow lakes and ponds, larger fish such as northerns prefer cooler, deep lakes. Anglers can find them near thick weeds in clear water. The best time for fishing for northerns is during the day when they feed. Their diet is mostly fish and sometimes frogs and other small water creatures. Using live minnows as bait works well. Northern pikes eat both live and dead animals.

Fishing for northerns requires a medium or medium-heavy action rod, 10- to 12-pound (3.6 to 5.4 kg) test line, a 6- or 12-inch (15 or 30 cm) leader, and a slip bobber. Anglers use spinning, spincast, or casting lures to catch northern pikes by trolling fast or casting. However, perhaps the most effective bait for catching northern pike is a spoon lure. These are bright, shiny, and made of metal. Spoons can be cast or trolled behind small boats at a fast speed. When a spoon moves through the water, it wobbles and flutters. A northern sees the moving spoon as live bait and furiously attacks it. Sometimes, the fish will follow the lure for a distance, striking it repeatedly before swallowing it. Fishers should set the hook after the northern has struck at the bait. Northerns have a hard mouth that can be hard to set a hook into. The spoons can be set with a very stiff or hard jerk.

Northern pikes will feed on dead fish that are on the bottom of a pond or lake. An interesting way to fish for northern pike in all seasons is by putting a large hook through a dead fish, and then using a weight heavy enough to take the bait to the bottom of a pond or lake. This method works well if the bait is an oily, small fish such as smelt, cisco, or lake herring.

MUSKIES

Muskies are long, heavy fish. They can be silver, light brown, or light green. They often have many dark spots on the body and smaller spots on the tail. Some muskies have no spots. All muskies have excellent vision. This fish can grow to 60 or 70 pounds (27 or 31 kg) and up to 40 inches (1 m) long in a large lake. Muskies can be found in warmer or colder water, shallow water, or deeper water. Their diet is mainly smaller fish that hide in vegetation, but they eat other live water animals as well.

Muskies are strong fish with very sharp teeth, making them a challenge to catch. Fishing for muskies requires 6-to-8-foot (1.8 to 2.4 m) baitcasting rods with stiff tip action and free-spool casting reels, lines of 20 to 50 pounds (9 to 22.6 kg), leaders, snaps, and swivels. Steel leaders must be used to withstand muskies' sharp teeth. Most anglers fish for muskies from boats by trolling and casting during the day when the fish are feeding.

Muskies put up a strenuous fight! Some anglers fish for muskies for the excitement and sense of accomplishment it gives them when the fish is caught. Many muskie anglers fish year after year and release every muskie they catch. They fish for the fun of catching this powerful and challenging fighter with a rod and reel.

When a fisher is casting, a muskie will occasionally follow the lure to the side of the boat. Then it will lie like a large, sunken submarine next to the boat. Suddenly, it will strike the bait if the angler loops the bait next to the boat in a figure-eight motion. Pulling in the vigorously fighting muskie is a thrill that anglers never forget.

Muskie, short for muskellunge, is a species of northern pike. They are a popular kind of sport fish in the United States.

RIVERS AND STREAMS

Most of the fish discussed to this point are most often found in lakes and ponds, but there are numerous freshwater fish that can be found in the rivers and streams of North America as well.

Bass are popular freshwater fish that live in all these types of water bodies and waterways. Largemouth and smallmouth bass can be found in large populations around the country. Both are known to put up a good fight, making them a target for sports fishers. Most people think the smallmouth bass is tastier. Another river bass you may come across is the spotted bass. The striped bass lives part of its life in the ocean but migrates up freshwater streams during the mating season.

The trout group includes several species of fish that live primarily in fresh water or may migrate to freshwater streams to mate. Trout are very similar to salmon, and it can be hard to tell the two apart. Both types of fish can be found in rivers and streams, and both are used to make delicious dishes.

There are about 2,900 species of catfish! Catfish can be found in many freshwater habitats, but most prefer shallow rivers and streams. Most are bottom dwellers, which means they live at the bottom of murky streams. The smallest catfish can be as small as 1.5 to 2 inches (3.8 to 5 cm) long. The largest can reach a length of 15 feet (4.5 m)!

Other freshwater fish that live in North American rivers and streams include carp, perch, and tilapia.

CHAPTER 4

AFTER THE CATCH

So, you've caught a freshwater fish...what's next? Catch-and-release fishing is very popular with casual fishers. However, others prefer to keep the fish they catch for eating because they can make tasty meals! Fish need to be kept alive as long as possible before filleting to make sure they taste good. If you can't fillet your fish right away, keep them packed on ice. Fish spoils rapidly if not kept cold, especially in warm weather. To keep fish fresh, anglers can let the fish stay in water on hooks called stringers or store them in a basket called a creel. Some boats have wells where fish can be kept alive until they can be filleted.

If you do decide to fillet your fish right away, be sure to do it in the proper location. Never throw fish scales or guts into the water, and never leave them lying around on the shore or deck. Many public fishing spots have cleaning stations with proper surfaces and sealed garbage containers. If these facilities aren't available, take the leftover guts home and dispose of them.

WHAT IS CATCH-AND-RELEASE FISHING?

Many fishers prefer to release the fish they catch rather than taking them home to eat or mount. In some fishing locations, fishers don't have a choice; they must return all caught fish to the water. In other areas, fishers must follow the regulations of the state and release fish of certain sizes, usually larger, older fish. Laws may require the release of these large fish because they are rare. In addition, they can breed, which increases the fish population of the lake or pond.

It is critical to release fish into the lake or pond as soon as possible to give them a good chance to survive. Fishers need to work carefully and quickly to remove the

This public fish-cleaning station on a pier in Sanibel Island, Florida, features a water pump, a covered refuse container, and a brush to clean up the area after it's used to clean fish.

hook from their catch. They should try to keep the fish in water, either by holding it or putting it in a net. To remove the hook, twist and pull it out smoothly using tools such as long-nosed pliers. When releasing the fish into the water, anglers should cradle its body, grip its tail, and slowly move it back and forth in the water. This allows water to move over its gills to revive it. When fishing in rivers and streams, you can hold the fish so the current moves water through the fish's gills. Then the fish is ready to be safely released.

It's important to be very careful when handling fish. Their gills are delicate and can be harmed easily. You can use barbless hooks to avoid tearing a fish's mouth. The fisher here is carefully placing this walleye back into the pond where it was caught.

CAN WE KEEP IT?

If you want to keep your catch, you should research state and local laws before you travel to any fishing destination. Fishers need to know the laws for the number of fish that can be stored in their possession at one time. Many lakes have daily fish limits and limits for what size of fish can be kept or released. This often pertains to older fish that still make new fish for future generations to enjoy. Other lakes have minimum size limits on certain types of fish to protect younger fish that haven't yet reached breeding age. The department of natural resources often posts these regulations at public accesses and fishing piers.

Every state has regulations on the legal possession limit for the fish of a lake, pond, or river. These laws are designed to prevent overfishing of a specific area. To learn about the fishing laws of a state, people can go to the state's department of natural resources website. The laws are also available every year at fishing license outlets, including county license centers, sporting and hardware stores, and bait shops. The money fishers pay for fishing licenses goes toward state enforcement of regulations. Game wardens enforce state fishing laws and check licenses to make sure people are not fishing out of season.

Many freshwater fishing locations post rules and regulations on signs at the site itself. However, you should still always research a fishing location before heading out. Some areas don't allow fishing at all.

CLEANING THE CATCH

It may seem gross to some, but knowing how to scale, gut, and clean fish is an essential skill for those who want to eat the fish they catch. The tools include scissors, a spoon or dull knife for scaling, a pocket knife, a fillet knife, containers for the cleaned fish, ice to keep the fish fresh, and newspaper for the discarded offal, or guts.

To start, anglers lay the fish on one side. Using scissors, they cut off any sharp fins. Next, they hold the tail or head and remove the scales on each side by scraping the spoon or dull knife against the skin toward the head. Now they are ready to gut the fish.

To gut, a sharp pocket knife is used to make a short cut near the anus on the underside of the fish. The knife is moved smoothly along the belly to the head. This allows a fisher to spread open the fish and remove the intestines and other organs. The fins, gills, scales, and intestines can be wrapped in newspaper and discarded. If you can't discard the guts at the fishing location, take them home to dispose of them properly. Never throw the guts or scales into the water or on the shore.

Next, the head and tail are removed. This leaves two fillets that are joined by the skin. To debone the fish, people use the tip of the filleting knife to cut and remove the ribs. Then they run their finger along the middle of the fillets to find and remove small bones. The skin might be left on or removed depending on the cooking method that will be used. The fillets are washed in fresh, cold water and cooked immediately. The fresher the fish, the better it tastes! Bigger fillets should be eaten within 48 hours. However, the thin fillets of panfish should be eaten within a day for the best flavor. They also may be preserved in the refrigerator or freezer.

LET'S EAT!

When properly prepared, panfish, walleyes, northern pike, and muskies are tasty and nutritious. Fish is lean and lower in fat and calories than many other types of meat. It can be prepared in many healthy ways such as grilling, broiling, panfrying, baking, steaming, and microwaving. Panfish are often fried in a little oil or butter. It only takes a few minutes to cook panfish. People also make fish broths, soups, and curries.

There are several ways you can cook your freshly caught fish at a campsite. They can be pan fried. The fillets can be cooked on a grill over an open flame. Some people use skewers to cook fish like this, especially for smaller fish.

FREEZING FISH FILLETS

Although fresh fish always tastes best, properly frozen fish tastes great too. There is a simple, inexpensive, and efficient way to freeze fish. First, clean an empty milk container made of waxed paper or a plastic jug. Next, cut off the top of the container and drop in fresh fish fillets until it's up to two-thirds full. Then fill the container with water so the fillets are covered and freeze them. Once the water has frozen, pour in additional water to completely cover any fillets sticking up through the surface of the ice. Mark the container with the date, type of fish, and number of fillets (or weight). This method of freezing fish surrounds the fillets in ice and keeps the fish fresh for up to a year. To use frozen fish, allow the fillets to thaw in the refrigerator. This is perhaps the easiest way to preserve fish. Other ways include smoking, dehydrating, and pickling.

Fish cooks fast, and it can be easy to overcook it. Overcooking will make the fish tough, and it may not taste very good. Fillets will break up if they are flipped, turned, or stirred too much during cooking. Fish is ready to eat when it firms up and gets flaky and opaque, which means you can't see light through it.

TROPHIES AND REPLICAS

Many anglers like to pose for a photograph with the fish they caught to show friends and family. It's also a reminder of a fun afternoon of fishing. They can take photos at the lake while they are fishing or when they are at home. If they want to catch and release the fish, the angler and photographer need to act quickly so that the fish can be returned to the water in a healthy condition.

Photographs of your catch can be enhanced by following some simple instructions. It's often good to take multiple photographs from different angles so you can choose the best ones. Make sure the sun or light source are behind the photographer's back. Before pictures are taken, an angler should take off their hat and sunglasses. Before snapping the picture, the photographer should have the angler hold their fish out in front of them, angling the fish's body toward the camera. This makes the catch look larger in comparison to the background in the photograph.

The photographer can make some other easy improvements in photograph taking. One is to fill shadows during the day with a flash. Most cameras set on automatic focus won't flash in the daytime, so the flash must be manually adjusted to go off. When focusing and framing a photograph or movie, you can take superior photographs by following the rule of thirds. This rule means placing the fish and angler at a location that is one- or two-thirds of the distance from either side of the camera's viewfinder. In addition, the photographer should focus on the face and upper body of the angler.

Would you like to have a large fish mounted as a trophy to be displayed on a wall in your home, cabin, or office? You can hire a taxidermist to prepare the wall mount. They will likely take photographs of the fish, handling it as gently as possible. Taxidermists skin the fish and cover a premade foam model of the fish with special glue. Next, they carefully stretch and fit the skin on the model and add glass eyes. Once the glue is dry, the skin is painted, and the trophy is ready to mount on a wall.

GRILLED PANFISH

This recipe can be made on a barbeque grill or over an open campfire.

INGREDIENTS

- four boneless, skinless fillets
- half a white onion, chopped
- 1 cup water
- 1 tablespoon pepper
- 1 tablespoon salt
- 2 tablespoons of butter
- aluminum foil, torn in 14-by-18-inch sheets
- lemon slices

DIRECTIONS

1. Preheat your grill to a medium-high temperature (400 to 450 degrees Fahrenheit).
2. Make a small plate out of the aluminum foil. Fold up the edges to keep the ingredients from spilling out. Butter the aluminum foil sheet and place the fillets in the center.
3. Add salt and pepper to both sides of the fillets and sprinkle chopped onion over them.
4. Add just a splash of water to the fillets to help keep them moist during the grilling process.
5. Garnish with lemon slices if you'd like, then seal up the packets.
6. Place them on the grill and cook for 7 to 10 minutes, flipping once. The meat should be white and flaky.
7. You can skip the foil and grill the fillets directly on the grill to give the meat a nice char if you want.

This muskie was stuffed and mounted to look like it is going after a fisher's lure.

What if you want to commemorate your catch without having to kill the fish? Instead of a trophy of the real fish, many people today are choosing fish replicas made of fiberglass. These models look the same as a trophy mount. Some taxidermists also make fish replicas. They will need to know some specific information, such as the length and weight of the fish. Take as many photographs as you can for the taxidermist to reference as they work. Like trophy mounts, replica mounts can be proudly displayed on walls to mark a great fishing memory for a lifetime.

CHAPTER 5

FISHING AND THE ENVIRONMENT

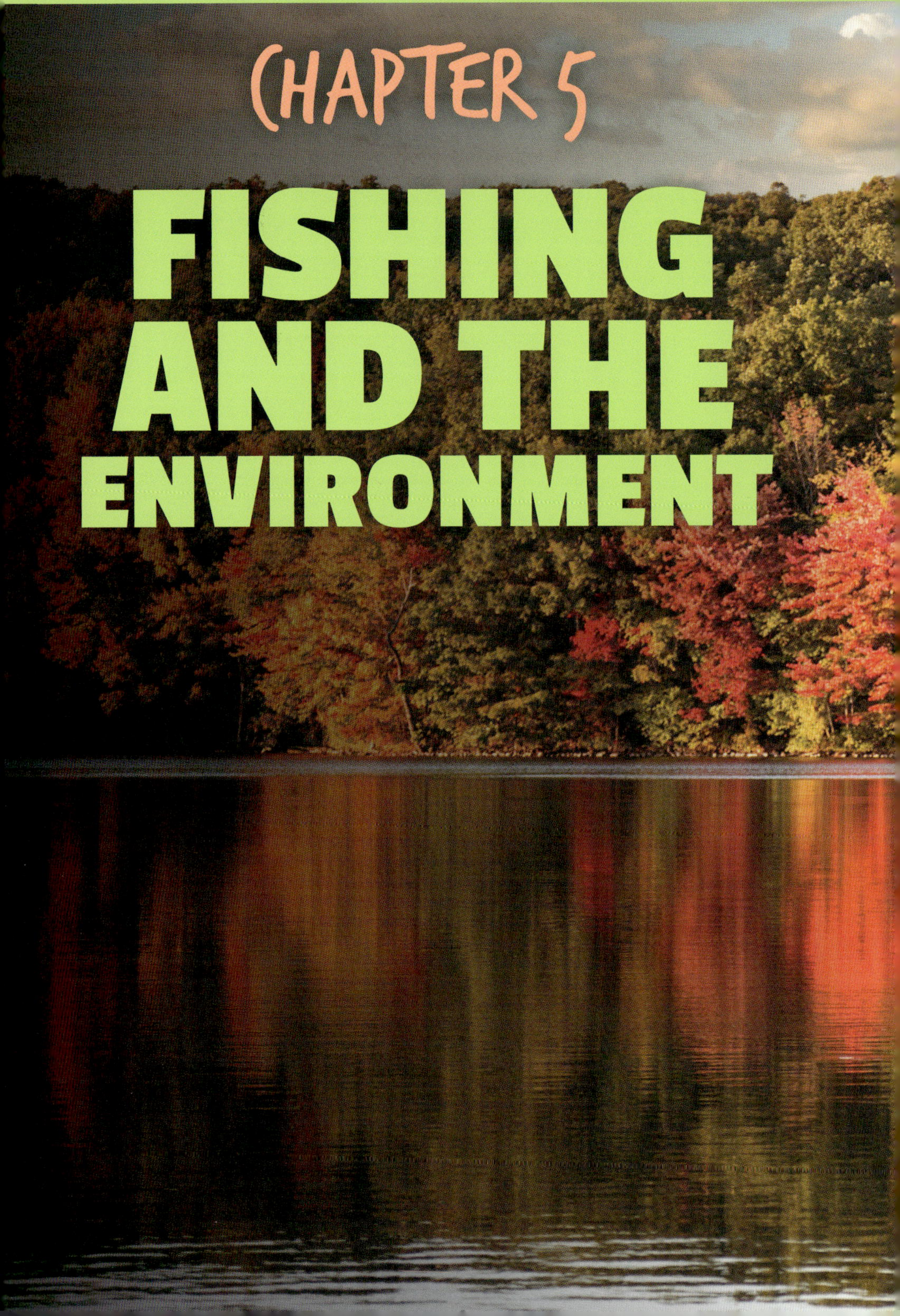

It's the responsibility of all anglers to keep fish and their habitats safe. Federal and state governments pass laws and regulations to keep the nation's water bodies and fish healthy and safe. States frequently conduct surveys of fish populations. They may construct man-made lakes and ponds that provide safe habitats where fish species can thrive. Both state agencies and the U.S. Fish and Wildlife Service share the responsibility of providing locations where citizens can boat and fish. Hatcheries are established in freshwater sources to help improve fishing by hatching and raising fish for stocking in lakes and ponds. States buy land and build boat and fishing piers to allow the public to access lakes.

HOW FISHING IMPACTS FRESHWATER ENVIRONMENTS

Fishing in freshwater lakes and ponds is a popular sport in the United States and Canada. Anglers spend hundreds of millions of dollars buying licenses, paying sales taxes on purchases of fishing equipment, and arranging for travel and lodging. States use some of this money to protect and replace fish populations and manage fish in lakes and ponds. For instance, they might stock fish in lakes and ponds if populations are decreasing.

It's true that fishing can provide enormous economic benefits to states and local areas. However, it can also negatively impact the environment. Overfishing threatens lakes and ponds. Bigger fish, such as northern pike and muskies, eat smaller fish such as panfish. If anglers take too many large fish, the populations of smaller fish can become too large. This makes it harder for them to survive as they struggle to find sources of food. Sometimes, anglers can overfish the smaller fish, which reduces the food supply for larger fish.

Freshwater fisheries raise fry and then release them into lakes and ponds to ensure future generations of fish will thrive. These catfish fry are soon to be released into the wild!

To keep overfishing or overpopulation from taking place, state governments set limits on how many specific types of fish can be taken from a lake or pond in one day. Some laws allow fishing only during certain times of the year. In some areas, people are prohibited from fishing during the breeding season because the fish do not reproduce if they are disturbed. Spawning fish come closer together than usual, which makes them far too easy to catch. Laws are put in place to prevent illegal methods of fishing, such as using spears or electricity. People cannot use nets that cause fish to get tangled in them and then die.

THE WATER POLLUTION PROBLEM

Water pollution in North America threatens the health and safety of people and animals. Clean water is essential for freshwater animals and plants. Power plants and factories that burn fossil fuels produce mercury that often finds its way into local water sources. This practice contributes to the pollution of lakes, ponds, and rivers. Mercury is a metal that is naturally found in tiny amounts in soil and rocks and can be released during weathering and erosion, so it's normal to find some level of mercury in local waters. However, large, toxic amounts can also be released into the environment from industries that use fossil fuels, such as coal. Mercury is very poisonous, and even small amounts can harm animals. Fish absorb mercury, and it builds up in their body over time. Larger fish eat smaller fish, and the mercury also builds up in their body. Too much mercury can cause fish and the animals and people who eat the fish to become ill and even die. This is why it's not a good idea to eat too many fish from the same body of water.

Button cell batteries, like those shown here, contain mercury. They are used in a large range of electronics. When these batteries or electronics are disposed of improperly, the mercury can pollute the land and nearby water sources.

GET THE LEAD OUT!

Lead is a naturally occurring metal used in the manufacture of some fishing equipment, including fishing jigs and sinkers. In the past, it was a common practice to paint lures and jigs with lead-based paint. If anglers do not know if their tackle contains lead, they should never put sinkers or jigs near their mouth. Some states restrict or ban the sale and use of lead sinkers and jigs.

Over time, the exposure of lead to a source of water can poison fish. Birds that eat fish, such as eagles, loons, and herons, are exposed to lead when they eat fish that have swallowed lead tackle. Other animals can be affected as well, including bears, wolves, and otters.

Anglers can help prevent lead poisoning by using nonlead fishing tackle. This equipment is made from nontoxic materials such as steel, tin, tungsten, bismuth, and copper. Never throw old fishing gear made of lead into the water, on the shore, or in the trash. These lead items should be brought to a local hazardous waste collection site for proper disposal.

Power plants often contribute to water pollution in another way. The heated water that these plants release into lakes and rivers reduces the oxygen in the water. Marine plants and animals die when there's not enough oxygen. Heated water can also negatively affect fish that locate their spawning areas by seasonal temperature changes.

Oil spills and chemical accidents also poison marine plants and animals. Agricultural runoff from large farms allows fertilizer and animal waste to enter lakes, ponds, rivers, and streams. Fertilizers help plants grow and are typically used for crops, lawns, gardens, and golf courses. Large levels of the nutrients in these materials can cause rapid growth of small aquatic plants. As more plants grow, other species die. Bacteria in the lake or pond use oxygen to break down the dead plants. They also use up the oxygen in the water. Without oxygen in the water, fish will die.

AN ANGLER'S RESPONSIBILITIES

As an angler, it's your responsibility to protect fish and keep their habitats free of pollution. Sometimes, careless fishers will throw trash into the water while they are on a boat or on the shore. People on a fishing trip might have old fishing line, weights, rigs, cans, and food wrappers. Misplaced hooks and lures can cause nasty injuries to unsuspecting hikers and to animals. Used fishing line is especially harmful to fish, birds, and other animals because they can get tangled in it and die. Anglers should put their trash into proper containers on the fishing site, or they should take the trash home and discard it. Some anglers take pride in cleaning up other people's discarded items to keep people, animals, and the environment safe.

Before fishing, make sure you're in an approved fishing area. Some lakes and ponds are off limits to anglers. Barbless hooks should be used. Fish that are caught with barbless hooks and then released have a better chance of surviving because barbed hooks easily damage a fish's mouth. They can also injure a fish's eyes, gills, and throat.

Anglers should only use approved minnows for fishing. Bait shops sell approved bait, but some anglers use unapproved bait. People who use goldfish and other fish from their aquarium as bait have caused the spread of invasive fish. When new fish are introduced to a body

Being a responsible fisher means cleaning up after yourself. Neglecting to do so can lead to injuries to people or animals. Plus, no one wants to look at your discarded garbage!

of water, the native fish often experience a decrease of populations. The local habitat can be damaged in several ways. Goldfish and carp are very harmful because they eat aquatic plants that reduce the level of oxygen in the water. As a result, water temperatures increase and native fish cannot reproduce. When they eat aquatic plants, goldfish and carp stir up the bottom of lakes and ponds, causing the water to become muddy. Many native fish cannot live in muddy water.

The snakehead fish is another invasive species affecting North American lakes. This fish comes from Asia and Africa and aggressively preys on local fish and small water animals. It can even crawl out of the water and move across land. An adult female snakehead fish can produce as many as 50,000 eggs at one time! This can make it very difficult to control this invasive species.

INVASIVE MARINE SPECIES

There are around 250 invasive species in U.S. water sources. These creatures were moved to the United States from other countries, and they flourished in their new environments. These invasive species compete with native species for food and space. Some are a threat to local people and tourists traveling to a fishing destination. Invasive species can greatly affect the natural processes in an area and usually require constant monitoring and problem solving. Sometimes, unfortunately, the invasive species wins.

Anglers need to take responsibility for the invasive species problem. Most important, anglers need to clean their equipment between fishing trips to avoid accidentally transferring species from one body of water to another. Boaters need to take similar precautions.

The common carp is native to Europe and Asia. However, it was introduced to freshwater sources in the United States to increase the species of edible fish available for fishers. Unfortunately, this has led to problems. The common carp is known to uproot plants and cause an increase in algae, which can harm native species and ruin habitats. This is just one of many invasive species that have caused problems in U.S. waters.

People should not release fish from aquariums or water gardens into lakes, ponds, or rivers. These fish could carry diseases that are deadly to the native fish. In most states, it is illegal to release nonnative fish into local water. If caught, people can be fined. They also may have to pay for the cleanup of the water.

THE NATION'S WATER

In 1972, the U.S. Congress passed the Clean Water Act to help control water pollution in U.S. waterways. This law set the guidelines that protect the nation's water by controlling the waste that companies put into it. The U.S. Fish and Wildlife Service manages and conserves fish habitats. This agency protects endangered fish and works to stop the spread of invasive fish. It also establishes wildlife refuges to protect fish and other animals. The public owns the fish in lakes, ponds, and rivers. Federal and state laws are put in place to control fishing to avoid overfishing and extinction of fish.

The National Fish Hatchery System, part of the U.S. Fish and Wildlife Service, protects and conserves fish by restoring fish populations that have decreased or died off in certain bodies of water. Fish are raised in hatcheries and then released into waters with low populations.

Dedicated anglers usually support laws that protect fish, improve their habitat, and increase fish populations. They buy fishing licenses, and some pay special taxes on fishing equipment. This money helps pay for enforcement of fishing laws, wildlife management, and conservation programs. Numerous fishers donate their time to help with wildlife management projects, such as improving fish habitats.

The Leavenworth Fish Hatchery was established to mitigate the environmental damage caused by the construction of the Grand Coulee Dam on the Columbia River in the state of Washington.

READY, SET, FISH!

Preparing for your next fishing trip should begin as soon as you come home from another fishing trip. It's important to clean and safely store fishing equipment. Check your rods for damage, sharpen hooks, and replace broken items. Many anglers keep a journal or online fishing log and write about what worked well and what did not for each fishing trip. They also note GPS coordinates or draw a map of where they fished.

There are many opportunities to improve your fishing skills and meet other anglers. You can sign up with a fishing club to learn how to fish more skillfully. Most fishing clubs have regular meetings, fishing days, and members who are willing to mentor beginners. Some clubs organize fishing trips to lakes farther away than the local fishing spots.

Books, magazines, fishing websites, and fishing forums on the internet can help everyone learn more about fish, fishing equipment, and methods for future trips. Check your local tackle and bait shops to discover great places to learn about fishing in nearby lakes and ponds. Plenty of people who work in these stores enjoy fishing and are often willing to talk about what fishing bait and equipment work best. Spending time freshwater fishing is a great way to have fun, meet interesting people, and catch fish that are delicious to cat!

GLOSSARY

chlordane A highly toxic liquid insecticide that was used in the United States.

conservation The protection and preservation of nature.

fiberglass A form of glass used for making various products.

global positioning system (GPS) A handheld computer that can calculate the exact position using a global positioning satellite.

graphite A form of carbon.

habitat A place where a living thing is naturally found.

hatchery A place where people allow fish eggs to hatch.

invasive Referring to a plant or animal outside of its home range and often causing danger to native species.

jig A kind of artificial bait that is jerked up and down through the water.

night crawler A large worm that is active at night on the soil surface.

sonar A device for detecting the presence and location of objects underwater by using sound waves.

spawn To breed when referring to fish, or to come together to make new fish.

spincast To fish with a light rod and reel that has a device that guides the line around a stationary spool and that can be disengaged to let the line run freely when casting.

taxidermist A professional who mounts trophies.

tension The pressure caused by the action of a pulling force.

trespass To unlawfully enter a person's property.

troll To fish by trailing a baited hook or lure through the water from a boat that is moving by a motor.

trophy A game fish or other animal that is suitable for mounting.

FOR FURTHER READING

Doyle, Abby Badach. *Freshwater Fishing*. Buffalo, NY: Gareth Stevens Publishing, 2023.

Hogan, Zeb, and Stefan Lovgren. *Chasing Giants: In Search of the World's Largest Freshwater Fish*. Reno, NV: University of Nevada Press, 2023.

Koestler-Grack, Rachel A. *Curious About Freshwater Fishing*. Mankato, MN: Amicus Learning, 2024.

Mazzarella, Kerri. *Freshwater Fishing*. New York, NY: Crabtree Publishing Company, 2023.

Reeves, Diane Lindsey. *Freshwater Fishing*. Minneapolis, MN: Lerner Publications, 2024.

Underwood, Lamar, ed. *1001 Fishing Tips: The Ultimate Guide to Finding and Catching More and Bigger Fish*. New York, NY: Skyhorse Publishing, 2022.

Werner, Robert G. *Freshwater Fishes of the Northeastern United States: A Field Guide*. Syracuse, NY: Syracuse University Press, 2023.

FOR MORE INFORMATION

American Sportfishing Association
1001 North Fairfax Street, Suite 501
Alexandria VA 22314
(707) 519-9691
Website: asafishing.org
Facebook: @ASAfishing
This group provides information about angling and the sportfishing industry.

Association of Fish and Wildlife Agencies
1100 First Street, NE
Suite 825
Washington, D.C. 20002
(202) 838-3474
Website: info@fishwildlife.org
Facebook: @FishWildlifeAgencies
The Association of Fish and Wildlife Agencies promotes fish management and conservation.

Fresh Water Fishing Hall of Fame and Museum
P.O. Box 690
10360 Hall of Fame Drive
Hayward, WI 54843
(715) 634-4440
Website: www.freshwater-fishing.org
This organization is the international headquarters for education and promotion of freshwater fishing.

Future Fisherman Foundation
5998 North Pleasant View Road
Ponca City, OK 74601
(580) 765-9031
Website: futurefisherman.org
The Future Fisherman Foundation works to introduce America's young people to angling and the outdoors.

The National Wildlife Federation
11100 Wildlife Center Drive
Reston, VA 20190-5362
(800) 822-9919
Website: www.nwf.org
Facebook: @wildlifeaction
The National Wildlife Federation works to protect and restore wildlife habitats in lakes across America.

Recreational Boating & Fishing Foundation
500 Montgomery Street, Suite 300
Alexandria, VA 22314
(703) 519-0013
Website: www.rbff.org
The Recreational Boating & Fishing Foundation works to increase participation in angling and boating and protect, conserve, and restore the nation's aquatic natural resources.

U.S. Fish and Wildlife Service
1849 C Street NW
Washington, D.C. 20240
(800) 344-9453
Website: fws.gov
Facebook: @USFWS
This government agency manages, conserves, protects, and enhances wildlife and their habitats.

INDEX

O

P

R

S

T

W

Z

ABOUT THE AUTHOR

Dwayne Hicks has written books for kids and teens for over 10 years. He has been on numerous family fishing trips with his father and grandfather—they particularly enjoy fly fishing. Hicks lives in Buffalo with his two dogs and an aquarium full of fish.

ABOUT THE CONSULTANT

Benjamin Cowan has more than 20 years of both fresh and saltwater angling experience. In addition to being an avid outdoorsman, Cowan is also a member of many conservation organizations. He currently resides in west Tennessee.

PHOTO CREDITS

Cover Krzysztof Odziomek/Shutterstock.com; pp. 4-7 (background) Rostislav Stefanek/Shutterstock.com; p. 6 Chekyravaa/Shutterstock.com; pp. 8-9 Monkey Business Images/Shutterstock.com; p. 13 gpointstudio/Shutterstock.com; p. 14 FtLaud/Shutterstock.com; p. 16 SlayStorm/Shutterstock.com; p. 17 Skrypnykov Dmytro/Shutterstock.com; p. 19 Pelow Media/Shutterstock.com; p. 21 Jesse Stephens/Shutterstock.com; p. 23 RossHelen/Shutterstock.com; pp. 24-25 OlegDoroshin/Shutterstock.com; p. 26 Nosyrevy/Shutterstock.com; p. 28 Air Images/Shutterstock.com; p. 30 (top) Smiltena/Shutterstock.com; p. 30 (bottom) Dewitt/Shutterstock.com; p. 33 FabrikaSimf/Shutterstock.com; p. 35 Tamakhin Mykhailo/Shutterstock.com; pp. 38-39 RLS Photo/Shutterstock.com; p. 40 CLP Media/Shutterstock.com; p. 42 FedBul/Shutterstock.com; p. 45 Kletr/Shutterstock.com; p. 48 Kimberly Boyles/Shutterstock.com; pp. 50-51 Dmitry Sedakov/Shutterstock.com; p. 53 BeeRu/Shutterstock.com; p. 54 Jennifer de Graaf/Shutterstock.com; p. 55 HappyAngel 888/Shutterstock.com; p. 57 Nata.dobrovolskaya/Shutterstock.com; p. 61 Nick Shoe/Shutterstock.com; pp. 62-63 Romiana Lee/Shutterstock.com; p. 65 johntallboy/Shutterstock.com; p. 66 Pixel-Shot/Shutterstock.com; p. 69 Gorlov Alexander/Shutterstock.com; p. 72 FocusFantastic/Shutterstock.com.